Butterflies and Moths

CONTENTS

© Aladdin Books Ltd

Designed and produced by
Aladdin Books Ltd
70 Old Compton Street
London W1

First published in the
United States in 1986 by
Gloucester Press
387 Park Avenue South
New York NY 10016

Printed in Belgium

ISBN 0-531-17027-6

Library of Congress
Catalog Card No. 86-80621

Certain illustrations have previously appeared in the "Closer Look" series published by Gloucester Press.

The consultant on this book, David Carter, is Senior Scientific Officer, Dept of Entomology, British Museum (Natural History) London, England.

Butterflies and Moths

DENNY ROBSON

Illustrated by
NORMAN WEAVER, TONY SWIFT, PHILIP WEARE AND KAREN JOHNSON

Consultant
DAVID CARTER

Gloucester Press
New York · Toronto · 1986

World of butterflies and moths

Butterflies and moths have existed far longer than we have. They first appeared 100 million years ago, whereas Man has been here for a mere five million years.

They are found almost everywhere, from sea level to mountain top, from Arctic tundra through the deserts of Africa and Asia, to the lush tropical regions where they are most abundant and brilliant.

Butterflies and moths come in a variety of shapes and sizes. The largest have wingspans of up to 300 mm (12 in), while the smallest pigmy moth has a wingspan of only 3 mm (0.1 in). And their colors are just as varied. In fact, no two butterflies or moths are exactly alike!

In this book we will look at the nature of this variety, the strange and wonderful life cycles of butterflies and moths and the ingenious ways they have devised to survive.

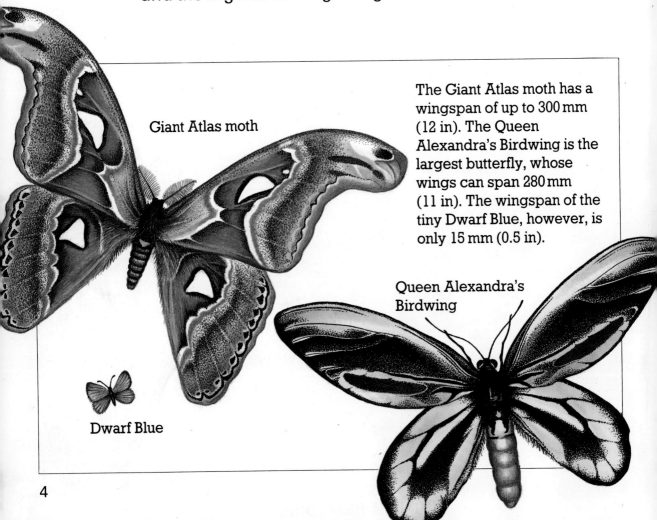

Giant Atlas moth

The Giant Atlas moth has a wingspan of up to 300 mm (12 in). The Queen Alexandra's Birdwing is the largest butterfly, whose wings can span 280 mm (11 in). The wingspan of the tiny Dwarf Blue, however, is only 15 mm (0.5 in).

Queen Alexandra's Birdwing

Dwarf Blue

Some hedgerow butterflies of northern Europe. Hedgerows are important habitats for butterflies and other insects. Their destruction is a threat to many species of wildlife.

Lepidoptera

Moths are often divided into Macrolepidoptera, (larger moths) and Microlepidoptera (small moths). Microlepidoptera include clothes and house moths.

Moths and butterflies belong to the insect order we call "Lepidoptera." Lepidoptera is the Greek word for "scale-winged" – moth and butterfly wings are covered with thousands of tiny scales.

There are far more moths than butterflies. About 145,000 out of an estimated 165,000 species of Lepidoptera are moths.

Characteristics of Lepidoptera

Lepidoptera have cylindrical bodies and two pairs of delicate and often colorful, scale-covered wings. They also have a complicated life cycle that goes through four different phases.

Among the moths belonging to the Macrolepidoptera are the large Saturniid moths, including this Emperor moth.

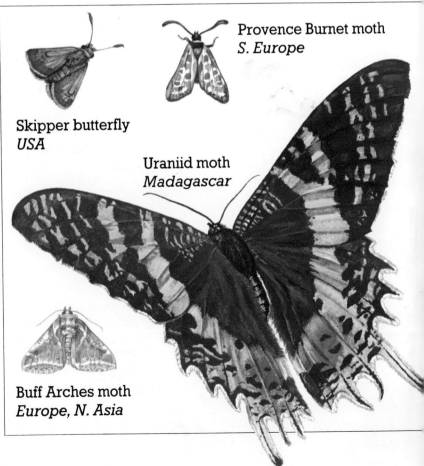

Provence Burnet moth
S. Europe

Skipper butterfly
USA

Uraniid moth
Madagascar

Buff Arches moth
Europe, N. Asia

Although butterflies are a relatively small division of the Lepidoptera, they are most frequently studied because they fly by day and are brightly colored. The Painted Lady butterfly (above) is a good example.

Differences

It is often difficult to tell the difference between a butterfly and a moth. But butterflies are usually "diurnal" (this means they fly during the day) while most moths are "nocturnal" (they fly at night.) Moths also have thicker, furrier bodies as a rule, and their wing colors are often dull.

Other distinguishing features are the antennae, which on a butterfly are enlarged at the tip to form "clubs," whereas those of a moth taper evenly or are feathered. When they rest, the wings of a butterfly are usually folded upright, while most moths fold their wings horizontally over their backs.

Union Jack butterfly
Australia

Brushfooted butterfly
Ecuador

Heliconiid butterfly
Peru

Brown Argus butterfly
Europe, N. Asia

Oleander Hawk moth
Europe, S. Asia

This random selection illustrates some of the differences occurring in moths and butterflies across the world.

Life cycle

Butterflies and moths undergo enormous and dramatic physical changes during their lives. Before they are fully grown, they must first pass through three distinct stages. They begin life as an egg, from which hatches the caterpillar, or larva, as it is sometimes called. This, in turn, changes into a pupa, or chrysalis, from which the imago – the fully-formed winged adult – finally emerges. The length of the life cycle varies. Some species have just one life cycle in a year, while other species have two or more.

Hibernation

Sometimes, because of changes in the climate, the onset of winter or the dry season, for example, the life cycle may be interrupted and no further development takes place for a while. This can happen at any stage in the life cycle, but when it occurs in the winter, it is called "hibernation."

The life cycle begins with courtship and mating. Mating couples, like the Adonis Blue (left) find each other by sight and smell, often performing elaborate courtship flights, chasing each other backward and forward over the same ground. When mating, butterflies and moths assume a tail to tail position, like the Poplar Hawk moths above.

Laying eggs

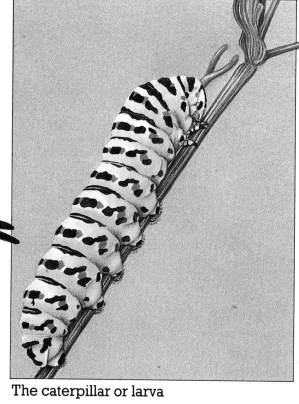

The caterpillar or larva

The pupa or chrysalis

The adult winged insect

9

Eggs and caterpillars

Lepidoptera eggs are about the size of a pinhead, and can come in many different shapes. They are usually white, cream or light green when first laid, becoming darker during development.

After hatching, the young caterpillars usually eat their eggshell before turning to the plants around them. However, some species are cannibals – they eat their own kind – while others will eat a host of unlikely substances, like wood and even other insects! During this period of voracious eating, the caterpillar grows very quickly. But as the skin of the caterpillar cannot stretch very much, it must be shed from time to time to allow the body to expand. Most caterpillars molt about four times.

Defenses

Some caterpillars have obvious means of defending themselves, such as stinging hairs or glands that squirt acid, but most simply hide among the foliage on which they feed.

Caterpillars, like those of the Large White butterfly, are made up of 13 segments plus a head. These are grouped into three thoracic segments, each bearing a pair of "true" jointed legs, and ten abdominal segments, some of which bear "false" legs.

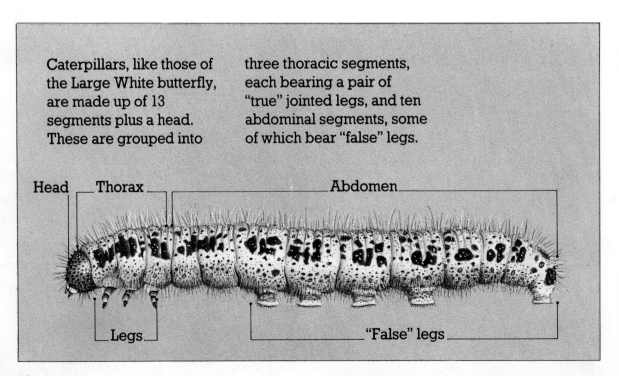

Head | Thorax | Abdomen

Legs | "False" legs

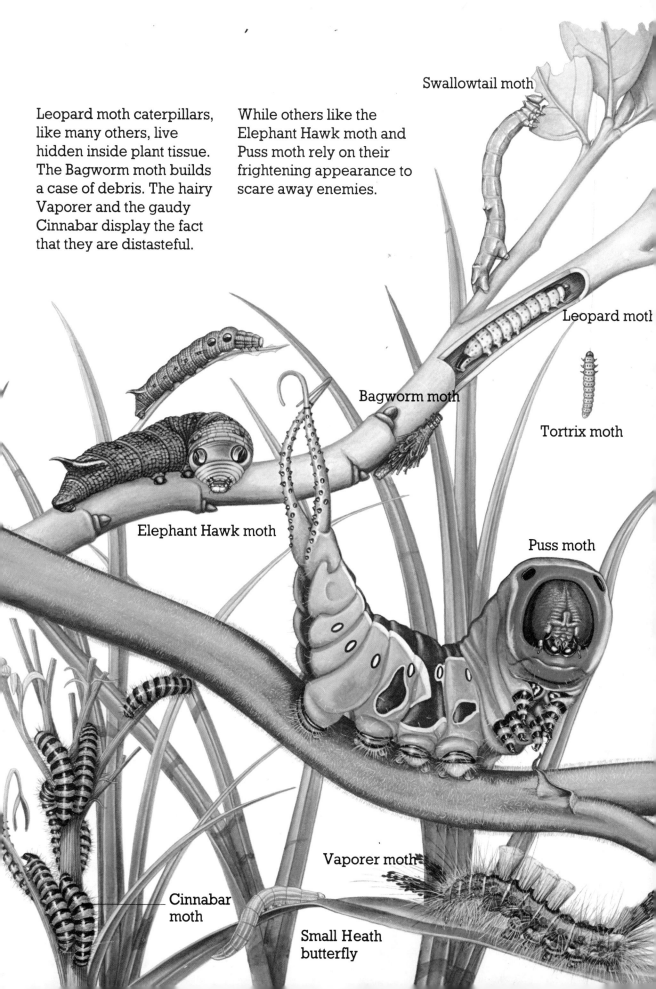

Swallowtail moth

Leopard moth caterpillars, like many others, live hidden inside plant tissue. The Bagworm moth builds a case of debris. The hairy Vaporer and the gaudy Cinnabar display the fact that they are distasteful.

While others like the Elephant Hawk moth and Puss moth rely on their frightening appearance to scare away enemies.

Leopard moth

Bagworm moth

Tortrix moth

Puss moth

Elephant Hawk moth

Vaporer moth

Cinnabar moth

Small Heath butterfly

Metamorphosis

Lepidoptera undergo a "metamorphosis," which means that the creature that hatches from the egg is completely different from the adult. When a caterpillar is ready to become a pupa it often changes color and its body contracts. It stops feeding, finds a suitable place, and then the skin splits for the last time revealing the pupa. This looks quite different from the caterpillar, and you can see outlines of parts of the adult butterfly (the eyes, antennae, proboscis, wings and legs) on the surface.

A Swallowtail caterpillar, right, spins a girdle of silk around its middle for support, sheds its last skin, and becomes a pupa.

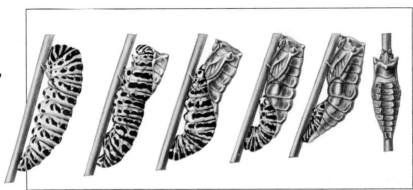

To protect themselves, many caterpillars bury themselves underground before pupating (1).

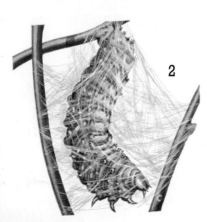

Moth pupae are often enclosed in a protective cocoon (2). Other pupae are camouflaged to look like their surroundings (3).

Swallowtail butterfly

Disintegration

Inside the hard shell of the pupa, some miraculous changes now take place. The tissues of the caterpillar break down into fluid form, and then are gradually built up into the organs of the adult butterfly or moth.

Emergence

When the changes inside the pupa are complete, the case splits, and the butterfly struggles out of the shell. At first its wings are only about one-tenth of their eventual size and are soft and weak. The insect must rest until they have expanded, hardened and dried.

A Japanese Swallowtail (above) emerges from its pupa (stages 1-4). Its wings having expanded and dried (5), it can now fly off in search of food and a mate.

The adults

The adult butterfly or moth, which usually only lives for a few days or weeks, is the final highly specialized and mobile stage in Lepidopteran development.

The body of the adult insect is divided into the head, the thorax and the abdomen. On the head are a pair of many-faceted, "compound" eyes and two long antennae, which help the insect smell and touch. The proboscis is a long tube used for sipping nectar, the usual food of butterflies and moths. Some moths, however, do not have a proboscis and so do not feed at all!

Thorax and abdomen

The thorax is divided into three segments, attached to which are two pairs of wings and six legs. One pair of legs has sense organs, with which butterflies and moths can taste and recognize the texture of the leaves of the food plants of their caterpillars. The abdomen has ten segments and contains the nervous system, intestines, reproductive organs and the "spiracles."

This is a Purple Spotted Swallowtail, on which you can clearly see the different parts of its body.

1 Head
2 Compound eye
3 Antennae
4 Proboscis
5 Thorax
6 Legs
7 Abdomen
8 Forewing
9 Hindwing

Coloration

The wonderful colors and patterns we admire in butterflies and moths are created by the thousands of tiny scales that cover the wing surfaces. The scales are arranged like tiles on a roof and they have short stalks that fit into minute sockets on the wing.

Pigment and structural color

Some scales contain a chemical coloring matter called "pigment." If the wings are touched, these scales can rub off on your hands, looking like colored powder.

Other scales contain no pigment, but they still produce color. This is because the way they are structured scatters light in different directions. This type of color has a metallic sheen. The gleaming blues and greens of many butterflies are structural color like this, and the color of the wings can change according to the direction from which they are viewed. Some Lepidoptera have light-reflecting scales that are also pigmented.

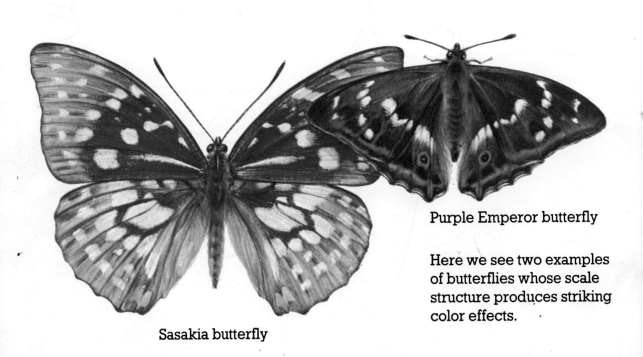

Purple Emperor butterfly

Here we see two examples of butterflies whose scale structure produces striking color effects.

Sasakia butterfly

Variation

There is always a range of variations in the colors and markings in any species of butterfly. Some vary very little, while others like these Chalkhill Blues have a wide range.

Species and subspecies

When butterflies or moths are geographically isolated, some differences become permanent. These two forms of the Apollo butterfly are subspecies.

Phases

The colors and sizes of some butterflies change according to season. The African Precis butterfly has very different coloring during the wet season (left) and the dry season (right).

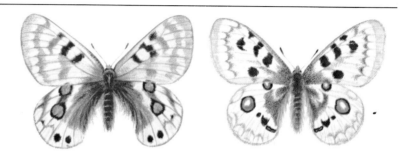

Australian Eggfly

When males and females of the same species look different we call it "sexual dimorphism."

The brilliant markings of these Birdwing butterflies make it easy for them to find each other.

Recognition and warning

The beautiful and varied color patterns of butterflies and moths help them to find mates. Each species has to be able to recognize its own kind. Lepidoptera see in color, and so, by being brightly marked, the males can identify females from other trespassing males by their different color patterns.

Color as a protective device

Color is also vitally important to the protection of Lepidoptera. Butterflies and moths are vulnerable to their enemies, particularly when they alight, and so they use color to create protective devices to avoid being attacked.

Poisonous and bad-tasting butterflies and moths use color to advertise themselves. By having very bright and bold color patterns, they can be recognized by their enemies as being inedible before they are attacked. Warning colors are usually red, orange or yellow, often with black or dark brown background. Insects with warning coloration often group together to create the maximum effect.

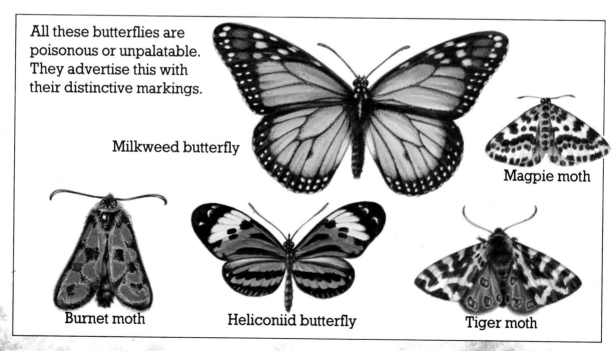

All these butterflies are poisonous or unpalatable. They advertise this with their distinctive markings.

Milkweed butterfly

Magpie moth

Burnet moth

Heliconiid butterfly

Tiger moth

Camouflage and mimicry

A major example of protective coloration is "camouflage," where the color patterns of an insect help it to blend into the environment and so hide from its enemies. Because butterflies rest with their wings folded vertically, the underside of the butterfly wing is colored inconspicuously. Moths, however, often rest with the upper surface of their wings visible and so it is the upper side that has the protective color patterns. When a tropical leaf butterfly alights on a branch of withered leaves, it seems to become virtually invisible. Moths are often camouflaged, by color and markings, to look like tree bark, so that they seem to merge into the tree to which they cling, and so can be unnoticed by their predators.

The markings of the Figure of Eight moth (above) allow it to blend into the grayish-brown bark of the tree. The Kallima butterfly from India (right) imitates a withered leaf so well that it seems to disappear when it rests on a twig.

These similar-looking butterflies are all of different species. They form a mimicry "ring." Poisonous species mimic each other and edible ones mimic the distasteful ones.

Mimicry

Another protective device is "mimicry," when a harmless butterfly or moth looks like an insect that *is* dangerous. Bees and wasps are avoided by most of their enemies because of their stings, and so some harmless Lepidoptera find it useful to imitate them. The Owlet moth imitates a spider, even moving its legs in a sidling motion.

Mimicking each other

Some edible Lepidoptera mimic others that are poisonous or taste unpleasant so that they too will be left alone by predators. Other butterflies, that are bad-tasting and so are avoided, mimic others that are also bad-tasting. By sharing the same color patterns, these butterflies reduce the number of times it takes for a predator to learn to leave a butterfly with their color pattern alone.

Bee Hawk moth

Alcathoe moth

Owlet moth

These moths above imitate bees, wasps and spiders in an effort to be avoided by predators.

A butterfly's day

Butterflies are usually only active during the day, although there are tropical butterflies that fly at dusk. Weather is very important to them. They are cold-blooded, like reptiles, so they must get their body heat from external sources. They warm up by lying in the sun with their wings outstretched, they cool themselves by finding shade and they shelter under leaves when it rains and at night.

Purpose

Although butterflies may seem to flutter around aimlessly in the sun, their movements all have a purpose. The main task of the adult butterfly is to produce the next generation and everything relates to this. They search for food (mainly nectar from flowers, but some butterflies also take food from rotting fruit, aphids' honeydew, tree sap and animal debris), but their main objective is to mate and lay eggs.

ECAR 78

These Postman butterflies of Central and South America have a predictable behavior pattern throughout the day. They begin the day feeding first on yellow flowers and then moving on to the red. Next, they find a partner and mate. Then the females lay their eggs on the leaves of the red passion flower, before returning to the yellow flowers to feed.

A moth's night

Moths are active mainly at night, so they cannot use the sun to warm up. Instead, they shiver their wings until their temperature is raised enough for them to be able to fly. Then, like butterflies, they fly off to feed, find a mate and breed.

Nightlife

Moths are particularly well-adapted to life at night. Unlike butterflies, they do not use sight to find their mates. They use scent, and each kind of moth has a different scent. Male moths have highly sensitive and often broad, feathery antennae, which can pick up scent from females up to 8km (5 miles) away. They navigate using their large eyes, which are very efficient. They can see in a different way from us. They are sensitive to ultraviolet light, which means that their night world must be full of colors that we cannot see.

Moths are attracted to light-colored and strongly-scented flowers.

In the foreground of the picture is a Clifden nonpareil moth avoiding a bat. It can detect the vibrations of the high-pitched sounds made by the bat with simple "ears" on the sides of its body. On the tree in the background is the Pale Tussock female moth, which is releasing scent to attract a male.

The Monarch butterfly of
North America, perhaps
the best example of a long-
distance migrator, travels
thousands of miles
every year.

In the spring, thousands of
Painted Lady butterflies
head north from Africa and
the Middle East into
Europe. Some of their
offspring return south in the
fall.

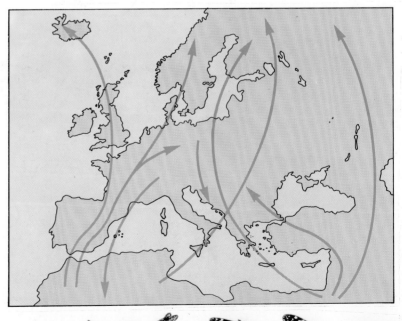

Migration

Some species of Lepidoptera "migrate" – they fly from one part of the world to another. The return flight, however, is rarely made by the same individuals, but by those of the next, or even later generations. Lepidoptera migration is not fully understood, but it seems likely that weather, changes in the environment, lack of food and overcrowding can trigger this phenomenon. Migration is a form of dispersal to ensure the survival of a species under difficult conditions.

The journey

Some cover remarkable distances, sometimes with thousands dying en route. Sometimes they arrive in enormous numbers and in other years only a few arrive. In bad weather and at night, they rest in trees in large groups. Records suggest that the direction and strength of the wind determine exactly where they end up.

Friends and enemies

Moths and butterflies can be useful. After bees and wasps, they are quite efficient flower pollinators. The silkworm is responsible for an entire industry. Silk moths are specially bred for the cocoons of silk fiber spun by the caterpillars when they are ready to pupate. Some plant-feeding caterpillars have been successfully used in weed control, by being artificially introduced into weed-infested areas.

Destructive pests

However, a number of species in the caterpillar form cause serious damage. Hungry caterpillars endanger crops, fruit and forest trees. Most farmers know about the destruction caused by the Cabbage White butterfly, whose caterpillar devours garden and field vegetables. However, moth caterpillars are more important as crop pests. Moths can also be serious pests feeding on stored food, the clothes in our closets, and in beehives.

These caterpillars are major pests in garden, field and forest.

Cabbage White

Codling moth

Pine Looper

Corn borer

Birds, like this titmouse, are common predators of caterpillars.

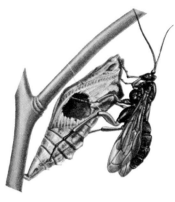

An Ichneumon fly emerges from the pupa of a Swallowtail, having destroyed the butterfly inside.

Enemies

Like other creatures, Lepidoptera have their enemies. They suffer from disease and have a host of predators. Birds, earwigs, spiders and wasps all take a toll of caterpillars, pupae and eggs. Spiders also hunt butterflies. A particularly unpleasant predator is the Robber fly, which attacks a butterfly in flight, and carries it away.

Parasitic insects

But possibly the most dangerous enemies of Lepidoptera are parasitic insects. "Parasites" are creatures that live either on, or in, the body of another animal. Lepidoptera parasites attack eggs, caterpillars, or pupae. Some live outside, but most are internal, like the grubs of the Ichneumon flies. Ichneumon flies lay their eggs inside the body of the caterpillar. The grubs hatch out and then feed on the caterpillar's tissues, without damaging the vital organs. The caterpillar is eventually killed, although sometimes it succeeds in reaching the pupation stage.

World without butterflies?

The numbers of butterflies and moths are sadly decreasing, and it is doubtful that there will be the same variety of species in 40 years' time as there is today. This would be a great loss.

Destruction of their habitat

Yet more deadly than their natural predators, people are contributing most to the decline of the Lepidoptera. Man is threatening their habitat everywhere. Wild areas are being cleared and replanted with agricultural crops. The atmosphere is polluted. Crops are sprayed with herbicides and pesticides. And with deforestation and soil erosion, these all contribute to the dwindling numbers of Lepidoptera. Several species, particularly those with highly specific food plants, are faced with extinction.

Butterflies and moths can be encouraged in the garden by planting nectar-producing flowers, like buddleia.

So what can be done?

On a small scale, we can protect them by not collecting butterflies, moths and caterpillars, and we can encourage them by planting nectar-producing flowers and suitable caterpillar food plants in our gardens. But ultimately, more of their natural environment will have to be preserved if we do not want them to disappear from our lives altogether.

Glossary

Compound eye An eye consisting of many individual lenses grouped together.

Deforestation The cutting down of forests or trees.

Extinction The dying out of a species.

Habitat A creature's natural home.

Herbicides Poisonous chemicals used for destroying plant life.

Nectar The sweet fluid produced by flowers, the usual food of butterflies and moths.

Pesticides Poisonous chemicals used for killing pests.

Pollination The sprinkling with pollen in order to fertilize.

Predator Creature that hunts and kills other creatures for food.

Proboscis A long tube formed from an insect's mouthparts that is used to suck nectar from flowers.

Spiracles Small breathing holes, situated along the sides of the body of an insect.

Index

PRINTED IN BELGIUM BY

proost
INTERNATIONAL BOOK PRODUCTION